33 Things To Know About Raising Creative Kids

Thank you around the world a million times to
Mason, Riley, Jordan, and Dane!
Your creative spirits have inspired me daily.

33 Things To Know About Raising Creative Kids

Whitney Ferré

TRADE PAPER PRESS

Turner Publishing Company
200 4th Avenue North • Suite 950
Nashville, Tennessee 37219
(615) 255-2665

www.turnerpublishing.com

33 Things To Know About Raising Creative Kids

Library of Congress Cataloging-in-Publication Data

Ferre, Whitney.
 33 things to know about raising creative kids / Whitney Ferré.
     p. cm.
 ISBN 978-1-59652-562-7
1. Child rearing. 2. Creative thinking in children. I. Title. II. Title: Thirty-three things to know about
raising creative kids.
 HQ769.F37 2010
 649'.51--dc22
                                          2009046890

Printed in China

10 11 12 13 14 15 16 17—0 9 8 7 6 5 4 3 2 1

The brain can be developed just the same as the muscles can be developed, if one will only take the pains to train the mind to think.

~*Thomas Edison*

When the artist is alive in any person, whatever his kind of work may be, he becomes an inventive, searching, daring, self-expressing creature. . . . Where those who are not "artists" are trying to close the book, he opens it, shows there are still more pages possible.

~*Robert Henri,* The Art Spirit

Contents

Introduction

Introduction

What does it mean to be "creatively fit," and why is it important for your children?

"The brain can be developed just the same as the muscles."

—*Thomas Edison*

The "creativity" described in this book is not inherited. It is inherent in every human being. This book's 33 simple things will illustrate how you can nurture and strengthen your child's creative ability. Encouraging this creative ability allows your child to become "creatively fit."

Your children have enormous mental capacity stored within their right hemisphere that can become weaker as they spend less time engaged in creative activity. Imaginative play is replaced with TV and video games. Coloring and drawing are replaced with writing and mathematics. The pressure to perform on standardized tests replaces "circle time." School becomes more about memorizing facts and figures and less about independent thinking.

Without an awareness of the importance of developing these right-brain mental skills, your young children can depart from their innate creative selves into logical, linear-thinking, left-brain-dominant "mature" individuals.

Whereas creatively fit individuals say, "We can make this work!" others may say, "It's never been done before." Whereas creatively fit adults interpret a job loss as an opportunity for positive change, others may feel defeated and depressed. How do we want our children to react to the obstacles life will inevitably throw in their paths? We want them to react with confident optimism. This self-confidence will come from their ability to envision the change necessary and, then, create that change! They will have maintained this self-confidence because you, their parents, learned how to keep both sides of their minds engaged and stimulated.

The Problem

Over the course of human history, we have proven ourselves to be very creative creatures. As human beings, we created art long before we created a written language or a monetary system. Thousands of years ago, in our most primitive state, we created extensive visual narratives on cave walls, on pottery, and inside ancient tombs. Ancient tribes created masks to summon powers from the spirit world to heal and to empower warriors in battle. Native Americans were "blessed" with a symbol that would remind them of their strengths and the skills they would need to survive the physical world. These symbols were painted on pottery and on their faces. They were woven into blankets. When the Native

American people were faced with challenges and hardships, these symbols would reinforce their will to survive and give them confidence in their ability to do so.

Only 200 years ago, a relative blip in the human timeline, we were intimately connected with the creation of every element of our environment. We felled the trees to make our houses. We raised the livestock that put food on our tables. If there was a problem, we had to fix it. We were creatively fit because our survival depended on it. Today we have become disconnected from our innate creative abilities. We don't have to create anything. We can order out, order online, and outsource almost anything. Where children used to have blocks and rocks, we now have bushels of toys, videos, and electronics.

That ancient, creative voice is still alive in the minds of our children, but we have to give it a platform. I have led elementary school students through a mask exercise to reconnect them with this voice and "work out" their creative muscles. I explained that primitive people created masks to invoke certain powers and abilities. We talked about the difference between the needs of ancient tribal people and our needs today. You could almost see their mental muscles stretching! When I asked them what kind of powers and abilities they needed today, they created "homework masks," "basketball masks," and, my favorite, "getting-along-with-my-sister masks." They loved it and it made a huge impression. I know they never looked at African masks the same again!

The Solution

This book is going to show you simply and quickly how to incorporate or preserve the necessary elements in your family's life to ensure that your children grow into creatively fit adults. Just as our muscles get stronger with physical exercise, so can we increase our children's, and our own, mental capacity to create. Remember that it takes time. You wouldn't sign up for a marathon and not work out ahead of time. You would understand that it takes months to get into that kind of physical shape, and that when you begin your training, you will not be able to run as far as when you complete your training. It is the same with our mental muscles. Each of these 33 Things are simple workouts you can do to raise creatively fit kids! Two important things to remember:

1. Your children are born with immense creative capacity. They already have it. You just need to help preserve it.

2. It is simple to do! With a very basic awareness, you can avoid the pitfalls that lead to a weak and ineffective right brain.

You will be amazed at the simplicity and ecstatic with the results!

A Simple Plan

This plan will provide the framework needed to create the change for your family to be creatively fit. It is not about right or wrong. It is about what little changes you can make to result in a big advantage for your kids. None of us are perfect. Don't think you have "failed" if one week, your kids end up in front of the TV a couple hours more than intended. Just keep taking the little steps, and as you tick off the 33 Things, you will sense the change being created.

Four Simple Steps

1. Mark a dot on the line next to each category to document your family's "creative fitness" level as of today (see next page).

2. Read *33 Things.*

3. Go to the final section of the book, 33 Things to Create Change Checklist, to check off the things as you complete them.

4. Then, after you have done each of the 33 Things, rank your family's creative fitness level (see next page) depending on how often you incorporate these into your routine. You will be amazed at how easy becoming creatively fit is and what a difference it makes.

Family Creative Fitness Level

We have art supplies readily accessible at our house.
Our family all the way!————————————Not us for now.

Our kids enjoy unstructured playtime every week.
Our family all the way!————————————Not us for now.

We limit time spent watching TV and playing video games.
Our family all the way!————————————Not us for now.

Our kids are great at entertaining themselves.
Our family all the way!————————————Not us for now.

Our kids' art is displayed at home.
Our family all the way!————————————Not us for now.

We often ask for our kids' opinions on a subject or event.
Our family all the way!————————————Not us for now.

As parents, we spend time on our own hobbies and interests.
Our family all the way!————————————Not us for now.

The 33 Things

~ 1 ~

Understand the potential within the right brain

— 1 —

Understand the potential within the right brain

Change is a constant in our society today. The need to access new sources of potential within us to create necessary change is more crucial than ever. New potential will be realized when we learn to bring the two hemispheres of the brain back into perfect balance. This new phase is shining light on the value of right-brain thinking so that our children can be architects of change.

There are other powerful voices in this Right Brain Movement, as I have named it. Dan Pink has written a best-selling book, *A Whole New Mind: Why Right-Brainers Will Rule the Future*. In it he warns us that the entire foundation of our economy is changing. Just as we moved from the Industrial Age to the Information Age, when the majority of manufacturing jobs moved to Asia, we are now moving from the Information Age to the "Conceptual Age." Many left-brain, task-oriented jobs are being outsourced to Asia, where the tasks can be performed just as well at lower costs. However, to stay competitive in this new phase, our industries need right-brain thinking, design, customer service, and innovation.

Consider the success of Apple. It was founded on multi-colored computer cases and hit its stride with shiny MP3 players that featured a simple, round control. Superior design set them apart from competition. Many businesses that failed in our latest economic challenge did so because their competition had superior customer service and design. Newspapers asked why Kmart struggles and Target continues to reach new markets. The answer? Target is "cool," Kmart is not. The "cool" factor is an interpretation of the right brain.

There has been a shift. The old paradigms that functioned in the Information Age are becoming outdated. Thus, we need to change the way we prepare our children for the future.

To guarantee that our children are able to "hit the ground running" as they enter the adult world, they must have knowledge of this "real-world" shift. They will need to be able to innovate new ways of doing things and design more appealing products based on what customers want, making that fit the bottom line rather than the other way around. They need to be able to see a project through from conception to completion without being micro-managed. Our country needs community leaders that can create grassroots change, government that can stay flexible and innovative, environmental engineers that can create new sources of energy, farmers that can maintain productivity without using chemicals, scientists and doctors that put the patient above drug companies, teachers and school administrators that can evolve teaching methods and standards, and individuals that move toward a brighter future because of their confidence in their creative ability.

In her book *My Stroke of Insight,* Dr. Jill Bolte-Taylor describes the different hemispheres of our brain. (Be sure to watch her presentation on www.ted.com. You will laugh; you will cry.) She describes how these differences became dramatically clear for her in 1996 when she suffered a stroke that left her with zero left-brain ability. As she was able to witness the stroke short-circuiting her left-brain abilities (she was a Harvard brain researcher at the time of the stroke), she was struck by the egocentric, fearful, stressed left-brain mentality as compared to the euphoric, loving, inclusive open mentality of the right brain. She illustrates how we can all choose to process situations in our lives from either a left-brain perspective or a right-brain perspective, with the goal being a whole-brain perspective.

Both perspectives are valuable, and to ignore either would be a waste. The right-brain perspective simply needs more publicity in our left-brain-dominated world. Its voice is drowned out by the up and down of the Dow Jones, the rising and falling interest rates, the foreclosures and bankruptcies. Continually scrolling through our minds is a to-do list, a barrage of details that needs attending, deadlines and responsibilities, finances, home repairs, computer maintenance, and technological challenges. Whew! It is overwhelming.

In order to not let routine completely consume our lives, we have to carve out some right-brain time so we can reconnect with our larger purpose, be thankful, reach out to others, and give attention to the artistry of living. Without that creative dimension, we become slaves to routine and wonder what we've accomplished at the end of the day.

Whereas the left-brain voice tends to be fearful and critical, the right-brain voice is generally supportive and filled with hope. Hope is directly tied to our confidence in our ability to create change. You are planting seeds of hope in the fertile minds of your children every time you take one of these simple steps to become creatively fit.

～ 2 ～

Provide unstructured playtime

− 2 −

Provide unstructured playtime

For most of us, childhood was a very different beast than it is today. We played cops and robbers outside throughout the neighborhood until dark. We rode bikes beyond our parents' peripheral vision. We built forts and tree houses, and an empty box was our own wardrobe to Narnia. We were not overbooked. We did not have afterschool activities, or at least not every day. No one had e-mails to answer or social networks to update. There weren't even cell phones! It was a much slower pace and left more to the imagination.

Today, the significance of "free time" is greater than ever. We are growing more aware of the value of open windows of unstructured playtime. As you clear your kids' schedules, bit by bit you will see their mental muscles start to stretch and flex.

When I was expecting my first child ten years ago, I read about the importance of allowing children to entertain themselves. The article said that even infants can learn how to entertain themselves. All the parents have to do is leave the baby alone (within their vision, of course) to soothe herself out of a fussy moment or to look around her without a toy shaking in her face or lights flashing around her.

As a result of reading that parenting tip, I would regularly give my new baby the opportunity to entertain herself. I remember sitting on the couch behind Jordan as she lay on a blanket on the floor. Initially, she'd move around and fuss a little bit, and then something would catch her eye. She would then quiet herself and become quite content. If I had scooped her up at the first whimper, she would not have developed that ability to entertain herself. The important thing she learned, even at such a young age, was to look within herself for entertainment rather than look to someone, or something else, to do that for her.

As my kids grew, I made sure to leave plenty of free playtime during which they would concoct elaborate dialogues and fantasies. My two girls had "imaginary college" when they were two and four years old. They would talk about, "When I was at college. . . ." We just went with it and marveled at their college adventures.

A few years ago, I found research by Teresa Amabile on the Creative Education Foundation Web site. She is a Harvard professor who has studied creativity, both in the corporate setting and in regards to children. What she found supports the importance of unstructured playtime: kids who were overscheduled suffered from the same type of stress her corporate clients experienced under time pressure. "Kids are best able to be creative when they have considerable free time," Amabile says. "Not glued to the television or to video games, but engaged in inventive play with other kids. There's too little of that. . . .

Get them out of this lockstep of one activity after another," she explains.

We can forget that kids don't need much to fuel their imaginations. All they need is some free time, a couple of blankets, a box, or just a willing friend. So next time you catch yourself thinking, "What should we do?" give your kids the chance to fill in the blanks. If they are older, make it a challenge: "Who can come up with the most surprising thing to do?" Then, give them a minute to switch gears, and watch the magic.

~ 3 ~

Turn off the TV

⊸ 3 ⊸

Turn off the TV

Today, kids can be driven by instant gratification and an aggressive extracurricular schedule. Cops and robbers has been replaced by Spy Kids on DVD. Dance class, tutoring, sports, and gymnastics have left little time for imaginative play. TVs are in cars and video games are easily accessible, so kids never have to entertain themselves. Remember when we were kids? There was usually only one channel with youth programming, and watching a movie meant driving to a theater! Times have changed.

After all, we as parents are so busy and so stressed that who could expect us to put up with a whining kid in the back of the car or in the kitchen as we attempt to prepare a healthy dinner, when they can be perfectly content plugged in to Disney? I have three children and multiple small businesses. I understand trying to keep your kids occupied while you work or have things to do. My work has also led me to enough information that motivates me every day to do at least one little thing to ensure my kids will be creatively fit. One thing each day will add up to a childhood dramatically different from the norm.

The good news is that verbal skills are a left-brain function. That means that if you give your children right-brain activities, they will become less verbal—less whiny. Instead of letting them plug into the TV, give them a coloring book, sketchbook, or sticker book. As they get into their drawing, they will become quieter and still provide you with the break you need to prepare dinner or do the laundry.

Here are some surprising statistics from www. kidshealth.org:

- Two-thirds of infants and toddlers watch a screen an average of two hours a day.
- Kids under age six watch an average of about

two hours of screen media a day, primarily TV and videos or DVDs.

- Kids and teens eight to eighteen years spend nearly four hours a day in front of a TV screen and almost two additional hours on the computer (outside of schoolwork) and playing video games.

Here are some more eye-opening statistics from the Web site of *The Sourcebook for Teaching Science,* www.csun.edu:

- Approximate number of studies examining TV's effects on children: 4,000
- Number of minutes per week that parents spend in meaningful conversation with their children: 3.5
- Number of minutes per week that the average child watches television: 1,680
- Percentage of daycare centers that use TV during a typical day: 70
- Percentage of parents who would like to limit their children's TV watching: 73

- Percentage of four- to six-year-olds who, when asked to choose between watching TV and spending time with their fathers, preferred TV: 54
- Hours per year the average American youth spends in school: 900 hours
- Hours per year the average American youth watches television: 1,500
- Number of murders seen on TV by the time an average child finishes elementary school: 8,000

So, try to think twice before your kids turn on the TV. It takes a lot of self-discipline for us as parents to restrict the TV, but it is one of the most powerful things we can do to help our kids develop the mental abilities they will need to be happy and productive in the future. If we help each other as parents, we could alter the landscape of these statistics dramatically.

My daughter came home from school a couple of months ago and declared that her friend Carter had decided to spend less time watching TV and more time reading. Wow! That made a huge impression on my daughter, who has been reading more as a result. I am grateful to Carter's parents for steering him in that direction! We can do that for each other.

~ 4 ~

Know the developmental stages of creativity

— 4 —

Know the developmental stages of creativity

I opened my first art center, the Creative Fitness Center, in 1996 in Nashville, TN. We quickly became the number one kids' art center, over long-time institutions and formal art schools. Needless to say, I got a lot of calls from parents. A common inquiry went something like this: "My six-year-old loves to draw and paint. She does it all the time, and I know that I am partial, but she is really, really good. So I want to enroll her in a serious drawing class to encourage her artistic ability." My first question would always be, "Let me ask you, is she still loving what she draws and paints? Is she proud of her work?" "Oh, yes!" they would say. I would explain that they are doing everything right by encouraging their child's artistic development, but that it was not time for serious art classes. Why? The risk is that at "serious" art classes, our young, enthusiastic artists can become discouraged and interpret the teacher's suggestions as meaning that the way they, the child, do it is wrong. That is a creativity developmental disaster!

When you are aware of the timeline of your child's creative development, you will be able to supply them with what they need to flourish and know when to supplement with outside resources. Every child is different, but the following breakdown of stages can guide you as you raise creative kids. (Go to www.learningdesign.com for more.)

1–2 years	Scribbling stage	Abstract, expressive
3–4 years	Pre-schematic stage	First "people" drawings, representative

5–8 years	Schematic Stage	Order in spatial relationships, scenes based on child's knowledge
8–10 years	Beginning Realism	Objects overlap, detail added, kids more critical of their work
10–12 years	Pseudo-Naturalistic	Kids increasingly critical, desire drawings to appear real
12–16 years	Period of Decision	Kids decide whether they are "artistic" and need to get over this hump with supportive, quality art instruction

I would recommend providing your young artists around ages seven to nine years with fun drawing books. (I write about this more in Chapter 16 about keeping blank paper around.) In that ten- to twelve-year stage a fun drawing class would be superb.

You simply want to be sure that the instructor has respect for each child's individual creativity. In other words, the kids should not be concerned with drawing exactly the way the teacher does. Kids need to feel successful in their art classes. A comment often made by the kids at the Creative Fitness Center was, "At CFC we are free to create the way we want!" If kids feel successful, they will be happy and creatively fit. For some to feel successful, they need to learn how to draw that cat exactly the way it is drawn in the book. For others, they need some basic guidelines or pointers, but then they go on their way. If you ask yourself, "Does my child feel successful?" the answer should guide you to the appropriate supplement that they may need.

Now, I can't emphasize enough the importance of persisting through these different stages. Try not to succumb to the paradigm that art is not important as the kids get older. If you can keep your kids feeling successful about their ability to create on blank canvas, they will grow into adults that will feel successful as they create change on the canvas that is their life! Is the real world more like a blank canvas or a multiple choice test? I rest my case.

— 5 —

Keep it simple

— 5 —

Keep it simple

I have met so many parents over the years that do not encourage art making at home because it is either messy or they don't feel that they have the ability to teach their kids how to make art. Good news! It can be simple!

All you need is blank paper, colored paper, crayons, markers, watercolors, scissors, glue sticks, a big plastic storage container, and a kitchen table. You do not need easels, canvas, acrylic paints, an entire studio, or any formal art training.

Remember, it is just like exercise. Your muscles don't distinguish between running around a state-of-the-art track or your neighborhood. You can perform bicep curls with cans of beans just as easily as you can with weights. It is the same with creative activity and your mental muscle. My kids have never had a fancy studio or private art lessons, just a corner of the kitchen table that they need to clean up before dinner, just like everyone else. Creating a composition on a blank page, whether it is a canvas or computer paper, using crayons or fancy acrylic paints, develops the same mental muscles. For your children to grow up to be creatively fit, you simply need to provide them with some kind of horizontal surface, basic supplies, and a supportive, non-judgmental cheering section!

The next time you are at a discount home store, buy a plastic box, some blank paper, markers, and crayons. Find a space under a table, on the counter, in the old play kitchenette, or in the closet by the back door and make that your family "art center." Pull out that container instead of turning on the TV, and watch your child's mind as it becomes creatively fit.

~ 6 ~

There is no such thing as a mistake

– 6 –

There is no such thing as a mistake

As a child, I remember getting frustrated when I colored outside the lines of the Shrinky Dink, or my drawing of a hippo did not look the same as the book's drawing. My mother was always quick to say, "There are no such things as mistakes." She may have been trying to smooth over a rough spot or dry my tears, but, to this day, when things don't go as planned, I am quick to move past the disappointment and on to the solution.

Certainly in the creative process, "mistakes" exist to help us understand our next step. Oftentimes, an artist does not know that the blue should not be the background color until the blue is put there. This is the creative process. This is the same with life.

We learn more from the challenges than from what comes easily. If we teach our kids to look for the potential within a mistake, we have given them a valuable tool that will help them to create success from failure, good from bad, love from hate, forgiveness from anger.

Look at Abraham Lincoln. He lost every election until he won the presidency. If he let those "mistakes" dictate his outcome, who knows which way history would have taken us.

When teaching young artists, I may see an improvement they could make or an additional step that would result in a more successful composition, but I never give them the impression that they have done anything wrong. I simply introduce them to new "tools" that they can use. They can then try the tools and decide if they could use them in the future.

There is always the parent in the group that harps on their child's "mud-making" ability: "All their paint always becomes brown!" "Don't mix all the colors together!" Another approach is to politely ask if you can show them how colors can go next to each other. Of course, the other equally valid approach is to let them mix mud, praise the heck out of it, and then when they ask you how to make red stay red, you will be ready to show them!

Our creative egos are fragile. There are very few creative actions that our kids could take that would result in irreparable mistakes. (Even the time my girls painted yellow and black paint all over the new carpeting was solved with a quick call to the carpet cleaner.) Let them paint mud and draw whatever suits their fancy. They are still working out their right-brain muscles!

— 7 —

Provide their teachers with creative resources

– 7 –

Provide their teachers with creative resources

Most teachers, whether in the private or public school sectors, are overworked and underpaid. They are multi-tasking constantly and have multiple demands on their time and energy. They are not all-knowing and never-sleeping (to keep up with all the latest information and trends, they would have to be!), and so they may welcome new input and inspiration. It does not hurt to express to them your desire to nurture your child's creativity, help them understand why that is important, and provide them with some resources they might find helpful.

I have been very encouraged lately to hear of many school districts supplementing their teachers' training with information about the importance of creative development. Entire school districts have purchased Dan Pink's book, *A Whole New Mind: Why Right-Brainers Will Rule the Future,* and Pink regularly speaks to educators. I also recently spoke to another huge creativity advocate, John Cimino of Creative Leaps International and the Learning Arts. For decades, his companies have been promoting to educators and Fortune 500 companies the benefits of including the creative process in all disciplines. He shared with me that most school curriculums compartmentalize the learning process by separating the subjects into unrelated tasks when, in reality, they are all related. Math, science, history, and reading do not exist on independent planes. John Cimino writes:

Learning is healing, growing, change. It is more than method, more than information. Learning is an affair of the heart as much as the mind. It is the linking of ideas and the creation of heartfelt meaning. It is the discovery of differences that make a difference and the re-assembly of the hundreds of "disconnects" we study into greater, more wonder-inspiring wholes. It is the "ah-ha" of self-recognition discovered in the poem, the flower, the equation, the just-revealed relationship with the world. Learning, in its essence and daily promise, is life-celebrating, life-sustaining, life-infusing, life-changing for both the teacher and the student.

Introducing your child's teacher to resources such as this, as well as www.learningarts.org, Dan Pink's *A Whole New Mind,* my first book, *The Artist Within: A Guide to Becoming Creatively Fit,* and the others listed in this book, can serve to inspire both your child's teacher and your child.

— 8 —

Ask them questions and let them solve problems

– 8 –

Ask them questions and let them solve problems

I read early on in my parenting career about the benefits of asking our children simple questions and letting them choose between a couple of possible solutions. This does not mean asking them, "What do you want for dinner?" This type of question leaves the door open for them to answer, "Ice cream and meatballs." It does mean that by giving them the opportunity to choose between baked chicken and quesadillas, you are allowing them to develop the ability to make good decisions and to feel a part of the process.

Likewise, regardless of our paths in life, we all have to solve problems. I remember reading in M. Scott Peck's book *The Road Less Traveled* that our personal success is a result of not how we handle situations when they come our way, but how we handle problems as they arise. If we are not given the tools to adapt to situations when they are not going our way, we will simply not be as effective in solving the problem.

We all know that real life requires constantly making decisions and solving problems. The task of making those decisions falls to us as adults. Our ability to make decisions, to act on those decisions, and to make productive choices is directly tied to our success, personal fulfillment, and effectiveness as members of society. People who have not been given the opportunity to make decisions through-out their lives are going to be more prone to wait-ing around for someone else to make decisions for them, not taking responsibility for their actions, and then regretting not following their own instincts. "It's their fault," "I did not know that would hap-pen," or "I don't know what to do" are not going to be answers that lead us onward and upward. "I can make this work," "I will take care of it," and "I need more information to make an educated decision" are responses that lead to productive activity.

As parents, we can overmanage our children and prevent them from learning these valuable skills. If we do not consciously give them the opportunity to share their input and contribute to solving problems, how will they learn these skills?

When your children become adults and face bumps in the road, do you want them calling you for money or a quick-fix, or do you want them to have the ability to accept their situations, assess their options, and take care of their needs? As an employer, do you look for staff that will need their hands held every step of the way, or for individuals who know how to act independently, take responsibility, and make things work?

All parents face the problem of children who exclaim, "I'm bored." The easy solution: turn on the TV. I consistently have to say, "TV is not an option. Would you like to play outside, draw, or read a book?" Teenagers are faced with very complex

— 9 —

Take them to museums

– 9 –

Take them to museums

We are all so busy, and it is easy to get into a routine. When you take your kids to a museum, it breaks that routine and wakes them up to a whole new world. Of course, exploring a museum can be fun for you too. Warning: kids may fuss a bit and say that they don't want to go to a museum. That is when you gently yet confidently assure them that regardless of their lack of interest or complaining, you are all going.

I was fortunate enough to grow up in Chicago, so I thought everyone had museums like the Art Institute of Chicago and the Museum of Science and Industry to go to. Even if you don't live in a major city, you should be able to take advantage of your smaller, local museums or make the point of visiting a museum when you are traveling.

Any museum, no matter how small, will have new information for your kids. It will present them with history, artwork, or knowledge that they would not otherwise have received. As a bonus, it is live! It is not on a screen—your kids are moving around and are engaged.

When I used to go to the Art Institute with my mom and brother, we would play a treasure hunt game with the works of art. We would divide up postcards of paintings displayed at the museum and split up to find them. Whoever got back to the meeting point first won. Of course, the thought of me running loose all over the Chicago museum at age eight is a little hard to imagine these days, but you can still find other ways to make a game out of your visits.

~ 10 ~

Get outside!

~ 10 ~

Get outside!

There is nothing better suited to expanding the minds and horizons of our children than the great outdoors. To the child who is creatively fit, the outdoors holds unlimited potential, forts, adventures, games, and fantasies. For others, it is more like being banished to the "Netherlands" at first. If given no other option, your child will make the shift (give them about five minutes) from the indoor world to the outdoor world. Just because they say, "I don't want to go outside," does not mean it is not a good idea. Insist that they go outside. Go with them. It will be good for you, too. Walk around the yard and point out interesting plants, shapes, and bugs. Get a bucket and a shovel and dig for worms. Play catch, swing, take a walk . . . do anything, but do it outside.

Here are other great ways to inspire outdoor time.

• Look up Andy Goldsworthy. Order one of his books. This man is an incredible artist who creates unbelievable art installations from all natural materials. He walks into the woods or another landscape with literally nothing and creates elaborate sculptures using only what he finds in the landscape. Kids love his work! After discovering Andy Goldswothy's art, my kids have stacked many a rock, constructed shelters from sticks and twigs, and seen a palette of colors in the fallen leaves. Extraordinary!

• A friend of mine, Rebecca Cohen, has a fabulous Web site at www.rebeccaplants.com with a wealth of resources for families to create quality outdoor time. "Something magical happens with me and my kids when we're outside and away from distractions," says Rebecca. "We listen better, we share and notice more about the plants and animals around us, and become closer as a family."

- Keep sketchbooks handy so that your kids can take them outside to draw plants, bugs, trees, and whatever catches their eye. My girls will do this quicker than my son, but it is always an easy activity to have ready.
- Go to a park, nature reserve, or hiking trail. My mom used to take us to the forest preserve so that we could climb trees. This was an activity we may have done only two to three times a year, but it made a lasting impression because we did it regularly. Hiking can be slightly painful the first couple of times, as the kids get used to the concept of long walks. The first time we took the kids to the local nature center, they took turns whining and fussing about how much their legs hurt, how they wanted to go back to the car, et cetera. It was not fun. However, by the second hike, only the youngest fussed a little bit (the kids were nine, seven, and five at the time), and by the third hike, we were all good. So, simply expect the first hike to be a little fussy and look ahead to the next hike!

ー 11 ー

Don't say, "I'm not creative"

~ 11 ~

Don't say, "I'm not creative."

Our kids pick up every single thing we say, and you are their plum line that they hold up to their own experience. If they hear you say, "I'm not creative," they are going to be more likely to repeat that themselves one day. The fact is that everyone is creative. Program yourself right now to understand and accept that you are creative. Expand your definition of creativity to include all the times you create change around you, which includes problem solving. The nature of a problem is that something needs to change that is not there at the moment, something that needs to resolve the situation. Your task is to create that change to resolve the problem.

I once received an e-mail with the following list, 16 Habits of Highly Creative People. I don't think it says a thing about being able to paint or draw.

From www.lifeahoy.sg
By Shalu Wasu, 26 August 2008

1. Creative people are full of curiosity.
2. Creative people are problem-friendly.
3. Creative people value their ideas.
4. Creative people embrace challenges.
5. Creative people are full of enthusiasm.
6. Creative people are persistent.
7. Creative people are perennially dissatisfied.
8. Creative people are optimists.
9. Creative people make positive judgment.
10. Creative people go for the big kill.
11. Creative people are prepared to stick it out.
12. Creative people do not fall in love with an idea.
13. Creative people recognize the environment in which they are most creative.
14. Creative people are good at reframing any situation.
15. Creative people are friends with the unexpected.
16. Creative people are not afraid of failures.

— 12 —

Shop for art supplies at the grocery store

~ 12 ~

Shop for art supplies at the grocery store

Think of art supplies as food for your children's minds. If they see you buying them markers, sketchbooks, glue sticks, and crayons at the grocery store, they are going to consider them just as important as the food you are buying. Also, you can get all the materials you need at the grocery store to help your kids become creatively fit. You do not need anything fancy.

Here is a shopping list in order of importance:
1. Sketchbook
2. Crayons
3. Markers
4. Glue stick
5. Scissors

6. Pencils
7. Watercolors
8. Glitter glue

You'll know you've made a breakthrough when the kids get just as excited about the new pack of markers as they do about a carton of ice cream!

~ 13 ~
Tie-dye

~ 13 ~

Tie-dye

Why tie-dye? Everyone loves to tie-dye. Even if you don't think you are part of that group, once you get going, your "inner camper" will bubble up, and you will be just as mesmerized by the resulting swirls and panels of color as your kids will be!

The other reason to tie-dye is that every time you wear your tie-dye shirt, it represents your creativity. You will all talk about the time you tie-dyed the shirt, and your kids will be so proud.

It is easy to find a kit at any craft store or online. Buy one this week and tuck it away for a nice afternoon when you can surprise the kids with this fun activity. You should already have old white T-shirts or pillowcases around that are perfect for this creativity workout.

Go to www.dharmatrading.com and order their Teeny Tiny Tie-Dye Kit. Dharma Trading is a company I have been ordering tie-dye supplies from since 1996. They know how to do it. Just follow the directions, and the colors will turn out bright and long-lasting. Have fun!

– 14 –

Volunteer in their art class

– 14 –

Volunteer in their art class

This may sound scary to you, but you will transform yourself into an instant artist in the eyes of your children and a superhero in the eyes of their art teachers. The more intimidating this sounds to you, the better idea it is.

Art departments, regardless of your child's education situation, are always struggling. It is complicated to lead a large group of students through a project, supplies are not cheap, and funding is always the first to get cut. If you put forth energy by just showing up to help cut, paste, and organize, you will be giving your arts program a huge jolt!

Another option is to recruit a local artist to come in to demonstrate his or her art and lead a simple project. The artist may be able to do this in your child's art class or homeroom class. Offer to promote the artist, his or her Web site, and the next art opening to parents at the school, and that should be all it takes. The parent-teacher organization at your school may even have a few dollars you could offer to pay the artist for his or her time. Some parents who are artists may be more willing to take the time if you offer to be the assistant. Anything is a help.

E-mail your child's teacher and ask if you can volunteer or coordinate a guest artist visit. Small efforts like these can come together to make a huge difference in your child's creative development.

~ 15 ~

Display their art

– 15 –

Display their art

When my oldest was just thirteen months old, I experienced the first look of pride on her face as she pointed to her pumpkins hanging in the kitchen. It was incredible. At the time, I owned the Creative Fitness Center and ran Mommy and Me classes regularly. I was the teacher and the participant as I always had Jordan with me. Because most of the kids were itty-bitty, I had to create some simple projects that would also result in sources of pride for both the itty-bitty artists and their parents. Our favorite was making garlands of their art to hang up depending on the season or holiday.

The first one we did was for Halloween. I simply cut out pumpkin shapes from orange construction paper, about one or two pumpkins per sheet. Then

I put red and yellow tempera paint on a paper-plate palette. (This paint is very washable and non-toxic, as is almost all paint.) Jordan had a blast mixing the colors to create different shades of red, yellow, and orange and slathering it on the pumpkin cut-outs. As the pumpkins were drying, I gave her a piece of black construction paper to tear into pieces. We then used those pieces to glue onto the pumpkins to create our jack-o'-lantern. To hang up the garland, we simply punched two holes with a pencil in the top section of the pumpkin and strung some yarn, twine, or string through all the pumpkins. I almost always had a garland hanging on the kitchen window or from the plantation shutters in the dining room. In fact, I think I still have a star garland (colorful paint strokes with drizzled glitter) from the winter holidays that has been up for years!

When you display your children's art, you are validating and celebrating their creativity. My thirteen-month-old Jordan who proudly pointed at her pumpkins and shouted some version of "Mine!" is the same as my nine-year-old Jordan who shows any visitors her artwork hanging around the house.

I have a friend who hung molding close to the ceiling in her front hallway so that she could hang strings with clips for her kids' art. She has about eight lines that create a wall of art and a dynamic installation in their home! There are hooks made just for this type of display, and fishing line or a more decorative ribbon with clips can be used to hang the art. Many home décor catalogs have fun display systems and picture frames that you can slide art into and out of for a rotating display. We have just used old-fashioned bulletin boards, special double-stick tape from the parent-teacher store, or the old "lean-the-work-against-the-window-sill" technique. In other words, anything works great! Just get the art up in the public eye so your kids know how much you love it.

Every time your children catch a glimpse of their artwork hanging in your house, it communicates to their subconscious minds that their work is important and valuable. The repercussions of that exciting thought programmed into their brains can be powerful.

~ 16 ~

Always keep blank paper around

~ 16 ~

Always keep blank paper around

It is just that simple. It can be computer paper, a sketchbook, construction paper, or watercolor paper. Coloring books, not so much. The reason is simply that you want your kids creating their own designs and characters, especially when they are young.

Now, as they get older, around six to nine years, it is okay to introduce some outside influences into their creative time. I often throw into the mix some simple drawing books. I don't ever talk about them needing to learn how to draw better or anything remotely similar; instead, I tell them, "Look at these books to get some ideas and learn some new things." The reason is I don't want them to think that the way they draw is wrong. I simply promote that they can learn some new tricks by looking at how other people draw.

I remember reading in Betty Edward's book, *Drawing on the Right Side of the Brain,* her musings about the way we teach reading and art. She hypothesized,

> What if we taught reading the same way as we taught art? We would just throw a bunch of books in the middle of the table and tell them to read. When a child happened to pick up reading on their own, we would inevitably say that the child did have a grandmother who was a really good reader.

Although we would never teach reading in this manner, we do much the same with art.

Kids can gain a lot of self-confidence when they follow along in a drawing book and draw an animal or face or alien that looks like it did in the book. The only rule is to not make it seem like you want them to learn to draw like the artist in the book. They have their own way of drawing just like we each have our own handwriting, but we still learn how to write letters very purposefully in school. The drawing books are simply another tool to help them stay interested and inspired in their creative activities. They also provide a great opportunity for you to sit down and draw with your kids. You will make a huge impression when you do this, and you will reap the benefits of the creative workout by engaging your right-brain muscles and becoming completely present.

You could pull out a How to Draw Bugs book and then go outside to find real bugs to draw. It is also fun to paint or draw a lot of designs and then tear or cut them up to make bug collages, a la Eric Carle. One thing will lead to another if you let it.

– 17 –

Introduce abstract concepts

- 17 -

Introduce abstract concepts

L ook back at that list of the 16 Habits of Highly
Creative People. Most of them have to do with
general curiosity and problem solving. Creative
people are open minded and thrive on a challenge.
They are not intimidated by the unknown or limited
by the way things have always been done. One way
to instill some of these habits in your children is by
talking with them about abstract concepts and ideas.

Here are some conversation topic ideas that will
be sure to stimulate both some confused expressions
and an open mind:
- The subconscious mind
- The importance of attitude
- Outer space
- Life in other cultures/periods of history

- "Lucky people are lucky because they believe they are lucky."
- The mind-body-spirit connection
- How plants grow
- The concept of "pay it forward"
- Success principles
- The power of visualization
- Goal setting

I have sat my kids down after school to explain that we have a mind, body, and spirit. I asked them to help me think about how much time we spent taking care of our mind (school), body (food and rest), and spirit (prayer, worship, and meditation). We reflected that we don't spend nearly as much time taking care of our spirit, but our spirit is closer to what is involved when we feel happy, sad, frustrated, or grumpy. We talked about what we can do to take care of our spirit: quiet time, helping others, being nice, and talking or praying. I am so convicted about the importance of spirit in the lives of my children if they are going to grow into happy adults. They can have all of the academic knowledge from school and enough food and shelter, but if they do not know how to take care of their spirits, they are not going to be happy.

This is pretty abstract stuff. Granted, I am sure a lot of that conversation went over their heads, but it was talked about. It will surely be remembered in some cell somewhere, and when they get older and outside of the realm of my influence, I am confident that snippets of these conversations will bubble up to their consciences and serve them in some way.

Again, creative people don't think they know everything because then there would be nothing left to create. They are open minded and confident in their ability to affect their environment. This makes them effective problem solvers. We want our kids to be great problem solvers when they grow up! Being aware from a young age that there are many different ways of doing things will create an expanded mind that is capable of processing a wide range of experiences and ideas. We tend to think that kids can't process this type of information, but their minds are really more open and fertile than those of many adults. Challenge them to think differently, to look at an event from a different perspective. Just explain what a "perspective" is—that is a creative workout right there!

~ 18 ~

Learn to draw a stick figure yourself

— 18 —

Learn to draw a stick figure yourself

If I had a dime for every time I have heard, "I can't even draw a stick figure," I would be rich! Let's take care of this objection once and for all. While we are at it—I don't believe there is such thing as a straight line either, so that one also won't hold water. Go ahead and admit it, you can do it!

– 19 –

Let them dress themselves

~ 19 ~

Let them dress themselves

A nother book that made a big impression on me as a young parent was *Kids Are Worth It* by Barbara Coloroso. She encourages allowing kids to be themselves in arenas that are safe; for example, clothing. As long as they are warm enough and not going to be at risk of indecent exposure, let them wear their stripes with their plaids and their layers of mismatched clothing.

Imagine what goes on in their minds. They are upstairs getting dressed, and after looking through all the clothes, they settle on an outfit that they think is really exciting. It has color, it contrasts. They come downstairs, some kids more timid, others beaming with pride, and you give them that look and tell them to go upstairs and put something else on.

You just shot the air out of their balloon. This is such an easy place to just let them be. Risk other parents seeing that you let your child dress himself. More often than not, it will inspire them to skip that battle themselves the next time their kid comes out in a crazy outfit.

One Halloween season my two-year-old dressed up as a cowboy. We could barely get him in his costume the night of Halloween, but then it took about three weeks to get him out of it. His favorite ensemble was the blue-suede, tasseled vest with no shirt on underneath (fortunately, it was a warm fall—I must have gotten a shirt on him for school, but I don't recall), his cowboy hat, blue shorts, and his sister's hand-me-down blue-and-white daisy rain boots! I remember walking through a department store with him in this exact get-up and leaving a wake of giggly older ladies behind us. I just thought it was hysterical. It was a ridiculous outfit, but he wasn't hurting anybody—and he loved it!

So when you can, let your children wear the tie-dye you all made in the backyard with the polka dot leggings or camouflage pants and the big hat! They are simply testing their independence and individuality—two things you want them to have when they grow up.

～ 20 ～

Don't buy video games

— 20 —

Don't buy video games

Is it really worth risking raising a child who grows up to spend hours and hours in front of his or her computer instead of engaging in the real world? The popularity of those virtual cities, or whatever they are called, is frightening. We have this entire population of adults spending hours daily creating virtual identities, in virtual towns, with virtual lives. Hmm, if they were happy with their own real lives, do you think they would be doing that? Most people retreat into fantasy when they feel out of control in their own lives.

It may seem kind of harsh, but I am convinced video games have a negative influence on our kids on so many levels. They shorten their attention spans, they make them crave instant gratification, they discourage their own creative minds by plugging into a world that has already been created for them, and they take time away from other productive activity.

This past Christmas, we bought my parents, who live eight hours away in Michigan, a Wii. They were actually thrilled, which was so funny to me, but the ulterior motive was to provide our kids with the opportunity to play Wii in a controlled environment, since we only visit a handful of times each year. So, we were heroes in our kids' eyes and my parents' and preserved our no-video-game zone in our home.

They are learning so much more valuable life skills by having to come to terms with the fact that they are the only kids who do not have such-and-such video games than they would if they had the games. My kids will get game time at friends' houses, don't worry. The time you have created for them to become creatively fit is ultimately far more valuable!

On the way to take my kids bowling one day, a friend in the car stated that playing bowling on Wii was easier than real bowling. My first thought was, "Yeah, I could have just found a friend with Wii and not had to go through all this hassle." Then, I imagined kids being nervous at the thought of actually having to perform an engaged, physical task. After all, at a real bowling alley you have to communicate with the adult behind the counter. You have to search the racks for the right ball—and those balls are heavy! Come to think of it, I look kind of funny when I am trying to bowl. It would be safer to just stay at home. Yikes! Why go swimming and get all cold and wet and have to shower and change clothes in a dressing room with strangers around? Why go hiking when you have to drive in the car and find a trail map and maybe get blisters or get lost? Why go down to the park to play basketball and risk looking silly and taking all the time, and having to put on a jacket, and the ball is just not as bouncy as it used to be?

Fast-forward twenty years. These same kids raised with a DS in their hands, Wii for exercise, and DVD players in the car are now faced with the busy, competitive world. This is not like a video game where you just have to learn the rules and press the right buttons. This is not a multiple-choice test. This is the wide-open, multi-faceted, complicated, messy, uncomfortable world!

Need I go on? Hopefully these images give you the resolve to stand tall and have confidence in your decision to encourage developing other skills in your children. You can do it!

~ 21 ~
Build forts

- 21 -

Build forts

This is a tried-and-true activity for almost any age! Whether it involves a tent or couch cushions, blankets, and a table, allowing kids to create their own space is giving them the opportunity to flex their creative muscles.

Save any large boxes. Let them and help them create windows and doors and decorate their clubhouse. Build a tree house in the backyard or let them sleep outside one night in the tent.

What they are really doing is creating their own space, their own environment. They are in control. They made it themselves. This type of experience reinforces their creativity.

One Saturday morning, my husband and I were in the kitchen and the kids were in the family room, just past the dining room and living room. We could hear them, but we had no idea what they were up to until we went to investigate. They had been busy building a "pond"! They had thrown over the second-floor railing every single towel, blanket, and bedspread to create the "water." They demonstrated what good swimmers they were by lying down on their bellies and flapping their arms. It was hysterical! We cringed at the shear mass of folding and putting away that was going to be required, but we were impressed by their imagination and willingness to alter the status quo. No harm done and a fun memory created.

~ 22 ~

Create your own holiday expressions

Create your own holiday expressions

Isn't it amazing how quickly the next collection of holiday paraphernalia appears in the stores just minutes after one ends? As soon as the back-to-school theme is past, the Halloween garb is jumping off the shelves. I joke about how hard it is to "live in the present" when it is only August and my kids are already bugging me for this or that Halloween costume or talking ghoul!

This year, pick a holiday or two and create your own décor, costumes, and celebrations. You don't have to be "Martha Stewart" about it. But set aside an evening or a Saturday morning to make ornaments, papier maché jack-o'-lanterns, or dye Easter eggs. At your local craft store, buy papier maché Easter eggs and glue collage items on them, paint, glitter, and sticker them, then gloss. They make a great centerpiece! You can get red, white, and blue fabric paint and some stamps to create 4th of July T-shirts. Good old-fashioned doilies, colored paper, glitter, and cut-outs make much more meaningful Valentine's Day cards and provide a great creativity workout!

When my kids were itty-bitty, I would cut stars, pumpkins, or shamrocks from colored paper. Then I would let the kids tear other paper into shapes that would make the jack-o'-lantern's face or the sparkle in the stars. I would give them a paper plate with two to three colors together (like red, yellow, and white for the pumpkins) and let them paint the shapes. When they were dry, I would string the items together to make a garland that would hang across a window or doorway. Polymer clay, like Sculpey, is another great medium to make holiday-themed table toppers. This colorful clay hardens in any oven and never dries out. The kids loved it!

Designer and writer Tamara Christensen shared with me a holiday tradition she and her son share every Christmas season: they create an "advent painting." On the first of December, they start with a blank canvas and add to it each day until Christmas Eve. She takes photographs daily and then assembles the photos into a book. Christmas Day her son gets to see both the finished piece hanging on the wall and the book that chronicles their collaborative experience. Go to www.creativelyfit.com to see examples of these paintings.

Keep it simple. You are teaching them to look within to create a special occasion, not outside of themselves to manufactured goods. They will get so much more out of the creative time together than they would during a trip to Walgreens!

～ 23 ～

Promote science

~ 23 ~

Promote science

I just attended a conference of the Creative Problem Solving Institute, the annual gathering for the Creative Education Foundation. We had the honor of listening to a presentation on "Innovation" by inventor and engineer Dean Kamen. Dean Kamen is owner of Deka Research and Development and founder of FIRST. He is our modern-day Thomas Edison.

Dean Kamen holds over 400 U.S. patents! He is the inventor of the Segway, the portable insulin pump, the portable dialysis machine, and a prosthetic arm named Luke (after Luke Skywalker) that is remarkably lifelike. He is currently developing portable energy and water purification systems for remote, third-world communities so that anyone in the world can have clean water. This man is creatively fit!

His proudest accomplishment is his creation of FIRST, For Inspiration and Recognition of Science and Technology. Mr. Kamen spoke passionately about the need for more positive and productive role models in our society. He argued that since professional athletes and Hollywood starlets get all the limelight, while scientists or "science kids" are more often portrayed as mad scientists and nerds, that our contemporary American culture has depleted our brain bank of future leaders and innovators who can solve the problems our world faces. He cited water and energy as the two largest problems facing our world today. Who is going to invent the new technology needed? Who is going to engineer the mechanics? The engineers in America are an aging population, quickly approaching retirement. There is not a large enough pool of young engineers to take their places. Currently, the United States hosts only six of the top twenty-four R&D/Engineering firms in the world.

Kamen sees an enormous lack of work ethic and desire to learn in our children today. He does not blame the schools. He says it is a demand, not supply issue, as we have talented, passionate teachers and adequate schools. Consider the average school in China, whose students study from 9 A.M. to 6 P.M. six days a week! He says that our teachers are not receiving diligent, dedicated learners. It comes down to our roles as parents to nurture and promote curious thinkers who value hard work and expect to work hard to accomplish great things.

To appeal to popular culture, FIRST created a sport out of science. They pair professional engineers with teams of youth to create robots to compete in the annual FIRST games, which last year packed the Astro Dome in Atlanta. Over 42,000 students participated from all over the world, and even a team from Africa participated in 2009. Sponsoring colleges and universities gave away $11 million in scholarships to FIRST participants.

Dean Kamen writes, "FIRST gives kids the opportunity to develop the muscle between their ears; to gain experience that will directly affect their future and our future as well."

We have a lot of problems to solve, and our survival depends on it. Without inquiring, scientific minds, we are moving towards a frightening future. Get excited about science. Expose your children to the field of science and challenge them to explore or invent solutions to problems.

There are several ways to encourage our future scientists. Check out library books about how people have invented solutions to problems. Buy them a microscope for a gift. We have a microscope handy for the kids so they can create slides from the insect wings, leaves, dirt, water, and other elements they find outside.

Subscribe to an age-appropriate magazine that promotes science. Look for science-related articles in the paper to talk about so that your children are aware of the tremendous role science plays in our lives.

You can also visit a children's science museum, or look for events at your nature center. Take a hike and talk about the food chain and ecosystems. Ask them about how plants grow from seeds or why the leaves change in the fall.

Although your kids are learning a lot of this at school, by talking about it at home, you are creating the opportunity for them to apply what they have learned. Science does not get our kids' attention as much as sports, entertainment, or computer games because it is not as widely promoted or is not made interesting. By talking about science more in depth, we are getting our kids excited about the opportunity they are going to have to contribute to their community and their world.

— 24 —

Have an easy storage system: start a "scrap album"

— 24 —

Have an easy storage system: start a "scrap album"

This is an easy one, it just takes the "doing." It is hard to know what to do with all of your kids' paintings, drawings, and creations. I think often we don't encourage our kids to create because we don't want to deal with the "stuff." However, several types of containers are available for your children to store their artwork in. My favorites are the big canvas boxes that can be ordered from a container store. Plastic storage containers, old trunks, or suitcases also work great.

For all of the drawings and smaller creative mementos, I keep a "scrap album." I am not a scrapbooker, but I have three-ring binders with the larger clear page protectors that are made to store catalogs. I label each one for each month and put twelve in each binder. Then, it is simply a matter of putting the drawings, art from school, random photos, and other items in the appropriate month's pocket. Just order several at a time, because it is amazing how the time flies!

You will find that if you have a system to store your kids' art, it feels much easier to encourage their prolific creativity.

— 25 —

Create a Web site for their art

~ 25 ~

Create a Web site for their art

This is so fun and easy once you get started. The result is an online gallery of your children's art that they can share with friends and family all over the world.

All you have to do is take digital pictures of your children's art and upload them to a photo gallery site. Our family uses www.shutterfly.com to create our sites. Let the kids do it—they may know more about it than you do! They can pick the site's background theme, colors, text to express artist statements, and inspiration.

Having an online gallery also reduces the need to preserve every piece of artwork the kids have created. That helps with storage. And if you e-mail your online gallery's url to our site, creativelyfit.com, we can share it with our community of readers!

− 26 −
Transform their art into product

– 26 –

Transform their art into product

There are many user-friendly sites where your children's art can be transformed into usable, giftable products like coffee mugs, aprons, mouse pads, calendars, T-shirts, and baseball caps. These sites include www.Cafepress.com and www.zazzle.com, which can design products and provide speedy delivery.

Your kids can also make their original designs available for others to order. Let them design a T-shirt to promote a cause or illustrate a change they want to see in the world, and then promote it online. Give them the opportunity to design their own "calling cards" to stick in birthday presents and teacher's gifts at www.overnightprints.com or www.vistaprint. com. Your children are becoming more creatively fit while gaining real-world experience and promoting a good cause.

─ 27 ─

Buy sidewalk chalk

~ 27 ~

Buy sidewalk chalk

Remember creating elaborate hopscotch trails and four-square courts on the school playground, or just drawing pictures on the sidewalk or driveway? Sidewalk chalk is sold everywhere, is inexpensive, and is an easy way to give kids a creative activity to do outside. Our kids learn so much from these types of simple, open-ended activities because what they create is entirely up to them. Read *Harold and the Purple Crayon* to them, and then give them the "magic tool" to create from their own imagination.

A fun parent/child activity is to go outside with your chalk and play a drawing game. Have your child draw something on the pavement, then add to it, then let her add something else, and continue taking turns. Before you know it, you will have an elaborate scene sprawling across the pavement—and you will have spent some quality time together.

Waiting for someone to come pick up your child for soccer or dance class? Take your chalk outside and play hangman or tic-tac-toe on the driveway. Your kids may be used to more advanced toys and games, but within that piece of old-fashioned sidewalk chalk is access to the infinite, creative side of their minds!

— 28 —
Have a family "paint jam"

— 28 —

Have a family "paint jam"

To create a fun family night, buy a large canvas and some acrylic paint. Put an old sheet on the kitchen floor and prop the canvas up against the wall or on the kitchen table. Put on some fun music and take turns covering the canvas. First, just cover the canvas with whatever colors, shapes, and lines anyone wants. Cover up all of the white. Does an object appear from within the scribbles of color?

You can also divide the canvas into a patchwork and have each person paint a design or object in each square. Paint a face in each square. Paint a flower in each square or paint flowers everywhere using different colors. Create an easy abstract painting by drawing a big, loose scribble line over the multi-colored background and then coloring in the different shapes created by the squiggle. Look at examples of Wassily Kandinsky's abstract work to get inspiration. You can keep painting on the same canvas for multiple paint jams until you love it! Don't forget to use some of your old acrylic house paint. It is a little drippier, but can be great for the base coat. Save the artist acrylic (just ask the art store for the best budget brand) for the following layers.

Hang your paint-jam painting somewhere you can all see it and add to it, such as in the kitchen or by the back door. Remember, it is not about the product so much as the time spent together working out your creative muscles.

~ 29 ~

Keep an art journal

~ 29 ~

Keep an art journal

This is easy to do. Just buy everyone blank sketchbooks. Write names on the front cover, decorate as desired, and leave them in a handy place so they can grab them while waiting for dinner or hanging out. Just date the pages occasionally and store them all in one box or storage container when they are full. If the kids come home and have had a rough day, ask them to draw a picture. They could divide the page into sections and document the day comic-book style, or they could create a storyboard. If they are more detail-oriented or left-brained, give them a pitcher or a shoe to draw. Just get them drawing. The voice in their heads reminding them of their past (left brain) will switch over to the voice that is totally present and void of ego (right brain) because they are doing a right-brain task. This even works with toddlers having a tantrum. Give them a crayon and their journal and ask them to draw a picture that you can hang on the fridge. By simply having an art journal handy, you are providing an extraordinary outlet, an alternate form of communication, and a creativity workout.

You can buy my favorite sketchbook, a Moleskine Folio Sketchbook, at our Web site, www.creativelyfit.com. The paper is nice and thick, and the pages lie open flat. These hip sketchbooks are available in many styles and are perfect for starting your kid's collection.

Taking a trip to the art store to pick out a creativity journal is a wonderful bonding activity for you and your teen. You and your kids can also visit a local bookstore and find published artists' journals. Inspiration is never far away!

~ 30 ~

Play mind games in the car

— 30 —

Play mind games in the car

I hate to beat the TV and video game thing to death, but they truly become a crutch so that children do not have to figure out how to entertain themselves. Do not even buy a car DVD player. If you already have one in the car, start to wean them from it. Put time limits on how long they can watch during a road trip. Do not let them be "backseat potatoes" the entire trip. I know this will make you unpopular, but we are not in the parenting arena to win popularity contests. We are here to raise our kids to be happy, productive adults.

My husband, three kids (currently nine, seven, and six), and I just drove from Nashville, Tennessee, to Northeast Oregon. We figured we covered 2,800 miles in fifty hours without an electronic game or

DVD player. They did emerge from the car at each gas station fairly covered in colored marker, but that wore off eventually. They made journals from notebook paper, they colored, and they played drawing games. I loved the game in which they took turns drawing people with their eyes closed.

Here are more of our favorite car games:

- *Alphabet game:* Find words that start with each letter in the alphabet, in order from A to Z.
- *Car bingo:* This oldie-but-goodie is available these days!
- *Initial game:* "I'm thinking of a person and their initials are . . . ." You can only ask yes and no questions.
- *Animal game:* "I am thinking of an animal . . . ." Again, only yes and no questions.
- *State capitals:* This can be tricky! I always need the atlas close at hand for reference.

— 31 —

Let them help in the kitchen and garden

‒ 31 ‒

Let them help in the kitchen and garden

Both the kitchen and the garden are great arenas for developing creative thinking, where kids have certain tools and ingredients at their disposal and understand that they are going to create something totally new from their efforts. A dinner you helped make tastes ten times better than one that was just plopped down in front of you. Some people say you can get kids to eat veggies, for example, if they help to prepare them. It hasn't worked for me so far, but I am still holding out hope!

When I was a child, my mom always let my brother and me pick out some seeds that we wanted to plant in that year's garden and included us in preparing the dirt, digging the holes, and, of course, weeding. Again, we were not always fired up to help, but we got such a thrill when the seedlings popped through the earth or the flowers bloomed for the first time. I did not inherit my mother's green thumb, at least I have not made the time to develop that particular skill yet, but we still make feeble attempts at the palette that is the backyard. This year my husband and each kid planted potatoes that had sat on the kitchen counter too long. One took considerably more time to sprout than the others, but they all grew into big, thick, green stems and leaves. The kids loved reporting each morning whose was growing higher. The sad ending is that they all withered and died suddenly (except one—we have yet to research when exactly potatoes are harvested), but the fun was shared by all!

In the kitchen, a fun kids' cookbook is a great tool. It might even get you out of cooking dinner a night or two! If you are not a big cook, start with cookies. Kids love baking. The recipes are pretty straightforward, and the results are a big hit! Another bonus is that the next time you go down the cookie aisle, your kids will be proud that they've made their own cookies. You are reinforcing that they can create what they need without looking to outside goods to satisfy.

～ 32 ～

Create a dream collage together

– 32 –

Create a dream collage together

This is another exercise that is so easy and can be done a myriad of ways to fit your own needs or personality. A dream collage is simply a collection of images that you like or would like to see in your future. Younger kids can include things they like, and the older ones can find things, places, or experiences that they would like in their future. Creating the collage can be as basic as pulling out old magazines and sitting around the kitchen table cutting out images to glue onto paper in an art journal, or assembling them on a posterboard or canvas together to create a family dream collage. One of our friends has created an entire dream collage wall for his family in their kitchen. It is like a big corkboard that covers a wall and is always a work-in-progress.

What a great way to promote to your family that you are the "artists" of the work that is your life together.

You could even create your own family dream collage album, much like the scrap album storage system I mentioned in Chapter 24. Make this activity part of your next family night, or just have a basket of magazines, scissors, and glue sticks in the middle of the kitchen table when the kids come home from school or get up Saturday morning. Instead of watching cartoons, create a dream collage! Then, take singer/songwriter Jack Johnson's lyrics to heart and "don't let your dreams be dreams." Believe in your dreams and believe that you can create the environment that will attract the right opportunities to turn dreams into realities.

— 33 —

Be aware of your desire to control

Be aware of your desire to control

We can unintentionally end up stifling much of our children's creativity because it is "not convenient" or is "too much work." We would be much more comfortable if we could control our kids to the point that there were no messes to clean up, no boo-boos to mend, or no feelings to be repaired. We would like to spare them from having to "learn the hard way." But we can't. We need to let our three-year-olds mix all the colors into brown if that is what makes them excited. We need to let them transform the family room into a pond by throwing down every single blanket, sheet, and article of clothing from the second floor (that was a funny surprise when my husband and I thought they were safely watching cartoons!). We need to give them the opportunity to express themselves with clashing colors and patterns.

Check yourself next time you want to say, "Don't do that." Could they really cause themselves or someone else bodily injury, or is your own inconvenience more likely the reason you respond with this command? If you provide your children with a safe, supportive arena within which they can explore their own creative abilities, you may have to sometimes sacrifice your own preferences or opinions, but you are encouraging and nurturing a much more vital quality: their confidence in their own ability to create the change they desire in their world.

So let go a little more to give your children room to wiggle, to try things "their way," to make mistakes, to solve problems, and, ultimately, to create the life of their dreams!

33 Things to Create Change Checklist

1. ☐ Understand the potential within the right brain
2. ☐ Provide unstructured playtime
3. ☐ Turn off the TV
4. ☐ Know the developmental stages of creativity
5. ☐ Keep it simple
6. ☐ There is no such thing as a mistake
7. ☐ Provide their teachers with creative resources
8. ☐ Ask them questions and let them solve problems
9. ☐ Take them to museums
10. ☐ Get outside!
11. ☐ Don't say, "I'm not creative"
12. ☐ Shop for art supplies at the grocery store
13. ☐ Tie-dye
14. ☐ Volunteer in their art class
15. ☐ Display their art
16. ☐ Always keep blank paper around
17. ☐ Introduce abstract concepts

18. ☐ Learn to draw a stick figure yourself
19. ☐ Let them dress themselves
20. ☐ Don't buy video games
21. ☐ Build forts
22. ☐ Create your own holiday expressions
23. ☐ Promote science
24. ☐ Have an easy storage system: start a "scrap album"
25. ☐ Create a Web site for their art
26. ☐ Transform their art into product
27. ☐ Buy sidewalk chalk
28. ☐ Have a family "paint jam"
29. ☐ Keep an art journal
30. ☐ Play mind games in the car
31. ☐ Let them help in the kitchen and garden
32. ☐ Create a dream collage together
33. ☐ Be aware of your desire to control

Check out these other books in the *good* things to know™ series:

5 Things To Know for Successful and Lasting Weight Loss
(ISBN: 9781596525580, $9.99)

21 Things To Create a Better Life
(ISBN: 9781596525269, $9.99)

35 Things Your Teen Won't Tell You, So I Will
(ISBN: 9781596525542, $9.99)

41 Things To Know About Autism
(ISBN: 9781596525832, $9.99)

51 Things You Should Know Before Getting Engaged
(ISBN: 9781596525481, $9.99)

99 Things to Save Money in Your Household Budget
(ISBN: 9781596525474, $9.99)

Contact Turner Publishing at (615) 255-2665
or visit turnerpublishing.com
to get your copies today!